ACTING WITH INTENTION

THE SECRET TO REDEFINING YOUR SUCCESS

SALLY ARKELL-BOLES & KRISTINE SALES

Order this book online at www.trafford.com
or email orders@trafford.com

Most Trafford titles are also available at major online book retailers.

Print information available on the last page.

ISBN: 978-1-4907-9368-9 (sc)
ISBN: 978-1-4907-9369-6 (hc)
ISBN: 978-1-4907-9370-2 (e)

Library of Congress Control Number: 2019901530

Trafford rev. 02/13/2019

www.trafford.com

North America & international
toll-free: 1 888 232 4444 (USA & Canada)
fax: 812 355 4082

CONTENTS

Preface vii

Chapter 1 The Home Party 1

Chapter 2 Discontentment 7

Chapter 3 Here's Where it All Starts 13

Chapter 4 Lunch Brainstorm Session 23

Chapter 5 It's Coffee Time 35

Chapter 6 Next Step—Debate 45

Chapter 7 It's Got to be Nonnegotiable 55

Chapter 8 Rev Up Your Engines 69

Chapter 9 Shorten Time to Success 89

PREFACE

You have been invited into real-life events. This book is a recount of the actual conversations held between two business partners as they discuss their personal experiences in coaching their sales team.

Sally Arkell-Boles and Kristine Sales are managing partners within a financial center. Their conversations were specifically focused on the needs of the advisors within their sales team.

What developed through these conversations is a wonderful coaching tool that keeps things simple and intentional. These pages will unfold for you the creative process in which the tool was developed as well as the conversations that ensued helping the two leaders reach these conclusions.

If you are in sales, or are interested in a strategy to help you reach your own specific goals in any life area, this success formula will help you focus on your own key deliverables while motivating these actions with passion and energy.

ONE

THE HOME PARTY

"Sally, you need to meet Kristine. She'd be perfect for our business. She'd make a fabulous advisor," Barb said.

I had just purchased a BMW and was headed to my friends' home for a direct sales presentation. I remember that night because my car and I were having fun testing out how fast I could accelerate from a red light. Now, the roads were quiet, my music was turned up, and I was singing rather loudly, "Life is a highway! I wanna ride it all night long . . ." I was in a great mood.

Barb had invited me as she was one of my best supporters and told me that I needed to meet Kristine and approach her about our business. You see, I was a recruiter but not in the typical head-hunting sense. This was an entrepreneurial opportunity that would require the candidate to study, apply for licensing, identify a client base, and complete market development as well as their financial and emotional investment to enter the business. Barb knew well the type of person it would take to be successful as she had been a successful advisor in our business for eight years. Barb saw something in Kristine that she knew I had to explore.

I arrived to find Kristine setting up her presentation. Of course, she was super friendly and happy and looked every part a professional salesperson. She lit up the room, and it was obvious to all of us that she loved what she did and was good at it. Kristine was in the beauty business, so we had to remove our makeup, clean off our faces, and get ready for some pampering. As the evening progressed, I could see she would easily make some sales. In fact, I bought the whole system *and* booked a party. I also watched her pick up a potential new sales rep or two. She wholeheartedly focused on her clients and added her product knowledge when needed. She was an expert at making everyone feel appreciated, beautiful, and welcomed.

Throughout her presentation, I was watching her intently and trying to find a way to approach her and have a conversation about our opportunity. Barb was a little less wary and just blurted it out—"Sally, you need to recruit Kristine!"

We all chuckled and went about our evening mingling and checking out the products available. At the end of the night, we made an appointment to meet for coffee. What I now know about Kristine is that she is always open to meeting new people and never says no to an opportunity to learn from others. Of course, she had also booked me to host a party at my home and needed to discuss the details.

A few days later, I met with Kristine for coffee. She told me she wasn't really interested in a new career but that she would hear what I had to say. I piqued her curiosity. I spent most of our coffee time learning about her business, how she achieved her success, what her goals were, and what she'd like to change in her current role. I discovered that the last piece was key; no matter how much success we are having, we all still have some thread of discontent. There is always something that we wish we could change in our current situation to afford us the luxury of having what we really want in our lives. Kristine was no different than I was before I had found this career.

TWO

DISCONTENTMENT

Like many women, I fell into a sales business because of family commitments. Just as I was coming off my last maternity leave, the private college I had been working in closed its doors. My knee-jerk reaction was to go back into the public school system as I was a certified teacher. This meant being on call, and I certainly wasn't keen on that idea. Three children, with two in diapers, and never knowing from one day to the next if I would be working—it was awful.

I was approached regarding a direct-selling business. At first, I was very adverse to the idea as I didn't feel I was "good at sales" and that being in this industry would cheapen my education.

Boy, was I wrong. Once I found my way, I was unstoppable. This decision changed my life forever. I very quickly started earning a large income. It took me only one full year to achieve a leadership role in the company. My first large paycheck was just over $11,000 per month. I had never dreamed of this sort of monthly income. My mind-set shifted, and over time, my idea of "normal" changed drastically. My new leadership role included recruiting and developing my sales force. I had the privilege of watching salespeople experience the kind of success they had only dreamed possible.

When I met Sally, I had been in this very successful direct-selling business for ten years. The first five years felt like the ride of my life. I quickly became one of the top producers in the company. Soon after, I took on a leadership role and began to climb the career ladder in record time. My new business offered many fantastic awards, including a red convertible Mustang and twenty free travel vacations to amazing locations like Paris. This company had really nailed the concept of compensation and recognition.

My success was recognized in many ways. I was loving my life. By nature, I am very results-driven, I gain a lot of self-esteem from my performance, and I am capitalistic in nature. I enjoy the challenge of continually increasing my income.

Our team was having record-breaking results, and it was fun when our leaders would meet. We all drove red convertible Mustangs, and this always made a scene. Parking all these hot cars would take up at least one full block.

In our sixth year, things unfortunately started to change. The company wasn't showing the same profit margins, and new corporate consultants were sent in to make changes and improve the bottom line. They started with overhauling the compensation plan and then made changes to the recognition system. The latter was the biggest blow to my team since all of us really appreciated the recognition that we had earned in the earlier years with our company.

Eventually, all our systems started changing, and with every change, my sales team would lose confidence. My business started crumbling around me. The morale on my team was low. In the first year that the company had changed the compensation, I lost twelve directors. This broke my heart, not to mention it drastically affected my income.

As the compensation and recognition were watered down, so was the energy of my team. I felt like I had lost control over my own career. Have you ever felt like this before, where changes that are happening around you affect your performance and that of your team? I was no longer feeling able to influence the results. We were not growing; in fact, we were going backward. I still had a good income and was considered very successful, comparatively speaking, but I began feeling like I was settling for less than life's best for me.

I had to make a big decision; was it time to move on? I began asking other career leaders out for coffee to discuss their opportunities. I felt that I should go back into a sales role, where I could control my own success again. Depending on my sales team had become a contentious topic for me. I was pouring my heart and soul into them, but they weren't driving forward like they needed to (and like I needed them to). I began to feel selfish and started asking myself, "Am I a good leader?" As the sales volume decreased, so did my self-confidence. I knew I needed to do something different.

THREE

HERE'S WHERE IT ALL STARTS

Had Sally approached Kristine at the right time? Yes. Could she sway her over to our company while she was still having success? Perhaps. Was her thread of discontent strong enough for Sally to influence her decision? Possibly, and Sally was up for the challenge. Sally had to find a way to attract Kristine. She was high-caliber and would be worth the effort. Her persistency paid off, and she was able to get Kristine to follow her firm's rigorous selection process. Kristine loved the experience so much, she joined the management team.

"Kristine, when you came into the management role, I was super excited to train you once again. I had so much fun training you the first time as an advisor. I couldn't wait to see the impact you would have as a manager."

"Yes. Truthfully, the memory of that excitement likely influenced me over to the dark side." Kristine giggled.

"Kristine, we both know that our success strategy worked with you," Sally said, "but how can we roll it out to all our rookie advisors? We need to create a tangible formula and test it out. Are you willing to help me with this?"

"Oh, I can't wait to help you with creating a duplicatable formula," Kristine said enthusiastically.

It all started one day as Kristine was talking with Sally, quite exasperated by a coaching session she had just had with a new advisor.

"Let's go for coffee, Kristine. You get to choose which coffee shop today. Let's get out of here for a while. It's time to get started with our creation of this formula we have talked about," Sally said.

"Great, I'll get my purse," replied Kristine.

The two settled in with their favorite drinks and pulled out their notebooks. After the first sip, they started chatting.

"Sally, you have often said we need a different way because we're in different times," Kristine said.

"I sure do, Kristine," Sally replied. "We are experiencing many changes in our industry as well as in the world, changes that affect not only how we feel but also how we react to change in our everyday responsibilities. Wouldn't you agree that the world seems to be moving at such a fast pace? It can certainly appear overwhelming at times."

"That's an understatement," Kristine said, rolling her eyes. "I see it every day with our advisors, struggling to keep up with the regulatory changes, new technology, and internal company distractions."

"I've witnessed many changes," Sally continued, "and recognize when we allow change to affect our actions and reactions, life and business can become very challenging. I couldn't agree with you more, Kristine."

"So much has changed since I left my last sales career, Sally," Kristine said. "These past ten years have had so much advancement, it is almost comical. When I first started in sales, we could literally approach anyone. We also e-mailed massive numbers of people and didn't need authorization or unsubscribe buttons. We also did all our invoicing with pen and paper. Now we dictate notes to Siri, and privacy laws are stringent."

"No kidding," Sally said. "I feel the same way, Kristine. People also loved meeting their advisors face-to-face. When

I started in this business more than a decade ago, my clients loved to meet with me one-on-one and enjoyed developing a relationship. Now I find people are more averse initially to getting together. They don't seem to be looking for ways or reasons to connect in person. Instead, they research online on countless topics regardless of the validity of the information or its sources. Sometimes they even just read a post on social media and jump onto that bandwagon. This is a double-edged sword. Clients often are more comfortable believing information learned online rather than from a person who has the specific expertise, education, and licensing. They even Google their medical concerns and self-diagnose without going to a licensed doctor."

"Years ago, when I started in sales, I did not even own a mobile phone. I made all my calls with a landline. Now my children don't even know what a landline is. It is crazy." Kristine chuckled. "People answered their home phones every time they rang without call display. It was easy to take an hour and make prospecting calls. People often took my call, or at the very least, they listened to their messages. Now I find no one picks up, and they certainly don't listen to their voice mail. I even know people who have applications on their smartphones that transcribe their voice mail to text messages. This creates a growing challenge in sales and finding effective ways to reach out and connect with even a warm lead."

"I see this change really affecting our new advisors, Kristine," Sally said. "There is no real-time conversation anymore. Sometimes our advisors get off track when their friends ghost their messages and take it personally that they might lose a friend because they've reached out to offer them their services. It can be frustrating and emotionally tiring to not be able to connect with your clients via conversation. We all know that text or e-mail can be misconstrued."

Kristine looked up curiously at Sally and asked, "Ghosting? Do you mean reading a message and not answering? I didn't realize they had a word for that."

"Oh yes," replied Sally, "and the newer advisors take this very personally."

"Sally," Kristine continued, "I was wondering if I could stay relevant with the rapid changes in social media and the e-business concepts. I am always best in front of people. I like people, and I like to be around them. I gain energy from having a live conversation. Being an online marketer is not something that I would have ever chosen to do. Regardless of how I feel, it seems this is the trend and the way a growing number of people are wanting to do business. Staying relevant in changing times can feel scary, and I see a lot of fear around this with our new advisors as well as the senior advisors."

"I totally agree, Kris," Sally said. "In today's changing times, it's really important to embrace the advancements that are happening around us. We must keep up with the speed in which these changes are affecting us personally and in our careers. We must *run* to keep up if necessary. Not only are we experiencing what seems like daily changes from regulators, but also, it's changing the industry landscape on how we manage our day-to-day business."

"When I started in our business, it was easy to get my licensing and head off to the races," Kristine continued. "In our industry today, the regulators are adding more work on our advisors to provide proof of education, attain designations, and document client communications to ensure that we're meeting standards. Once we're in the business, the regulators watch everything that we do and ask us to do additional paperwork to support every suggestion and decision that we make. All this is fantastic quality control for our industry. However, it certainly adds to our workload."

"When I joined our organization more than a decade ago," Sally said, "I was impressed by how many tenured advisors there were in our organization. As a matter of fact, I had never, in my whole career, seen as many tenured long-term advisors in any organization I had worked for. That's why I knew I could make this into my lifelong career should I choose. I had finally found the opportunity to create a business within a leading company, a career that would allow me to help others in the community but also develop my career until I choose to retire. Today the same tenured advisors are struggling to put together succession plans. There's a big gap between those advisors who are twenty-plus years in the business and those who are coming into the business. It's becoming increasingly difficult for senior advisors to find that successor for their business who will be able to continue to offer the same level of service to their long-term clients."

"No doubt about it, Kristine," Sally replied. "Change is the norm in a fast-paced society. Not only that, but also, there are so many changes politically. There's so much upheaval in our political environment these days, and the world is very small compared with what it used to be twenty years ago. The pace of communication, the information flow that's happening, is really affecting all of us daily."

"My daughters are always teaching me about the advances in technology," Kristine said. "Most of us are just learning one set of technology when another is introduced, and we need to relearn to keep pace. Now this is exciting. We love to be able to learn new things and expedite our successes, but at the same time, for others, it can be a bit overwhelming. Automation is also on the rise and is making a big impact on our careers and those of others around us. There are jobs created because of automation, but there's also a lot of jobs that are being sacrificed for automation."

"*Wow!*" Kristine exclaimed. "Sally, when we sat down today for coffee, I had no idea of the amount of change around us every day. You are right. The speed of change and our environment is affecting our sales team."

"Absolutely," Sally said. "I'm glad that we had this coffee break today. We need a new way for what we're facing, a simple focus on key deliverables. We need to look at a better approach that will shorten our time to success. By shortening that time to success, we really will make an impact on how many clients we can help have success in their lives. Kristine, I'm really looking forward to digging into this at our next coffee meeting. Let's put some thought into it so that we can help our team create a *success formula*."

FOUR

LUNCH BRAINSTORM SESSION

Later that week, Kristine had come into Sally's office for a meeting.

Sally put her agenda aside and asked Kristine, "What is it that makes you successful in sales?"

They knew that there had to be a way to put their process into an easy formula and make it repeatable for everyone. They wanted to make sure that others would truly understand the impact this could have on their sales, their business, and their future growth.

"I think if we are truly going to brainstorm on what makes me successful in sales, we should go out for lunch, Sally. How does Thai food sound?" Kristine asked.

"How did you know that I was craving Thai food?" Sally replied. "Go grab your notebook too as I think we will come up with some great ideas to create a tangible success formula."

They arrived at their favorite Thai restaurant. Sally ordered her favorite pad thai, and Kristine ordered a delicious yellow curry. The smells in the restaurant were filled with aromas of exotic spices. As they were waiting, out came their notebooks, and the conversation started right away.

"Kristine, we are both high performers, and we both have successful careers," Sally said. "We both excel at development of sales people and training. As a matter of fact, we both love to teach."

"I know. Teaching is so dynamic yet can be very challenging at times. What I am wondering now is, why am I having a challenge with my new advisors creating success like I experienced?" Kristine mused out loud.

"Good question, Kristine," Sally said. "When I was training you, you were very clear on your income-generating activities, but I'm not sure that our current advisors have defined what those activities are in their business."

"I completely agree, Sally. What seemed easy for me doesn't seem quite as easy for them. Thinking back, what were my income-generating activities?"

"Before we met for lunch," Sally started, "I asked you, 'What is it that makes you successful in sales?'"

Their meals arrived, and they both started enjoying their lunches.

"Let's think of it this way," Sally continued. "See these onions in my lunch? We need to peel back that onion layer by layer to get to the core of what really makes someone successful in sales."

The two started to brainstorm and write things in their notebooks. It wasn't easy. They even disagreed at times. They were straight and honest with each other, and sometimes they would argue about the points mentioned. It soon became very clear to both women that they had to define what are the critical income-generating activities. The key thing that they discovered was that people who succeed focus on activities that produce sales and income. It's not about what they wear, think, or say; it's about taking action.

"Sally," Kristine said, "I am interested to discuss why some people stick to sales and why others don't. I truly feel it's a sense of identity that must exist in the salesperson. It's important that if we're involved in a career where we're offering products and services, one should own the idea that we are in sales. I find when I'm working with advisors who are struggling, I normally discover they're in an identity crisis. They like to skirt around the identity of being in sales."

"I totally agree, Kristine," Sally said. "What I've found is that advisors like to talk about helping people solve problems and explain they believe in the 'soft sale' approach and often talk a lot about being relational. I think anyone who has been involved in mentoring or coaching people in sales can relate to these experiences."

"I understand why the verbiage is important, especially from a professional perspective, Sally," Kristine said. "This needs to be paired with a strong sense of purpose. At times these thoughts reflect a lack of confidence and project a sense of insecurity in the role. It may even represent a denial around what activities develop an income for them. If someone I'm working with is in denial about how they produce a paycheck, they avoid the activities that create their income. This is a fundamental problem that is not easy to overcome."

"This issue is definitely one that causes us as coaches to focus on self-discovery to investigate their *why* as well as their *how*. Once they decide to sew the two together, they will discover what is holding them back from success. Is that what you are saying, Kristine?" Sally questioned.

"Yes," she said. "I think that as we investigate the human aspects of selling in a world that is becoming technology-based and client-centered, we will be able to create our success formula. I find that advisors who are struggling with an identity crisis are the very ones who do all the activities that are not producing an income. They keep themselves busy but hide in unproductive work."

Sally quickly agreed. "We've all seen that, Kristine. It is one of the most frustrating elements of being a coach and a trainer. Advisors who are very clear on their identity tend to be much more focused on their income-generating activities. When an advisor becomes comfortable doing those activities that produce a paycheck, the activities feel less painful, and they will elect to do them more often."

"Advisors who struggle with this sales identity crisis and the very activities that produce a paycheck find themselves experiencing pain. Why?" Kristine asked but then offered her own answer. "They are not taking full ownership or feel a connection with those aspects of the business. The purpose of the success formula is to focus on the human aspect of a business owner to ensure that they're embracing their entrepreneurial identity. When I've seen advisors not utilizing this process, it's like running around with a blindfold on. The magic behind the success formula is that we can remove the blindfold and create a clear path to follow."

"Like you, Kristine," Sally said, "I like to have a lot of truth talk with a struggling advisor. Before I start to explain our success formula, our conversation will be around the concept of being in sales and the value that this brings to other people. I like to have candid conversations about their perspectives on sales and how they see themselves as a salesperson. The more we talk about it, the more they own it and the easier they're able to establish their own style and identity within the role. This is very foundational and necessary before we can move forward."

"You know, Sally," Kristine said, "I have my own story about my journey in identifying myself as a salesperson. In my first career, I was a teacher, and I was very proud of that role. I felt that I was respected in the community. When I went into my first selling role, I had a very hard time accepting this as a part of my activities or my professional identity. I know for certain I am not alone in this. I can remember a time when I was heading to a conference in Dallas. I was driving across the border, and the crossing guard asked me what I did for a living."

"'Kristine Sales . . . You must be in sales,' he suggested with a smile.

"I said, 'Oh no, I'm a teacher.'

"'Oh, so why aren't you teaching today?' he asked.

"'Well, I'm a teacher on call,' I replied.

"He proceeded to ask me why I was heading down into the States, so I told him that I was going to a conference for a direct-selling company.

"He looked at me as if I was a liar and said, 'So Mrs. Sales is actually in sales!'

"I was so embarrassed and replied haltingly, 'Well, yes, I guess I am.'

"I thought about that conversation for a long time as I drove down Interstate 5. I later promised myself that I was going to own this new identity and embrace who I was becoming. I decided that I was very proud of the fact that I was offering my clients something that they needed. I had already experienced how grateful my clients were after those interactions. I very quickly understood that if I was going to be successful, I needed to embrace the role. I know for a fact that it was on that very day that I said yes to success and never looked back."

"Kris, you are so right," Sally said. "I was very fortunate in my past to be able to coach an advisor who was really struggling with his own personal identity in sales. He had worked globally in the past with success. When he had arrived in North America, he felt less valued and even struggled with his name in this country. His name is Charles. He had tried to recreate himself as Chuck. I was coaching Chuck and noticed how he was struggling to find success in sales. I also noticed that Chuck was very animated and sometimes a little bit off-putting to most people. It seemed to me that he was acting how he thought Chuck would be expected to behave in his new country."

"During one of our coaching sessions, I decided that I needed to transform Chuck back to Charles. Charles was successful in all his past careers and had been respected in the community, and he was a professional resource for others. He also loved that he was a go-to person when a tight deadline needed to come to fruition. That gave him energy and a feeling of worth. Charles had lots of sales experience but somehow set that experience aside in his new role as an advisor. At the end of our meeting, Charles felt that he could now let go of Chuck and focus on bringing Charles back into his new business. I was awestruck by the actual physical transformation I had seen when Charles reappeared. A completely different person was in my office at the end of our meeting. How powerful it is to truly find someone's true intention and help them come back or discover the true intentions that relate to their success. In the weeks that followed, our team noticed a change in Charles's attitude and his sales activity as he embraced his 'old self' again."

FIVE

It's Coffee Time

"It's coffee time, Kristine. Let's go. We need to talk about our income-generating activities," Sally said.

"I'll be right there. Let me get my notebook," Kristine said, heading back to her office.

They left the office and went back to their favorite coffee shop.

Sipping her latte, Kristine said, "Sally, everybody who gets involved in a selling career has the exact same opportunity for success. So why do some have more success than others? Are elite producers simply luckier than other advisors who come in and fail? I often hear advisors talking about successful people with a little bit of jealousy or trying to come up with a reason why that advisor is more successful than they are. Everybody comes in on an equal playing field with the same opportunity and environment. There really are no excuses."

"I notice that even advisors who aren't getting the results appear to be working hard," Sally said. "They are putting in a lot of time, but are they focusing on the right things? I think we need to help them in determining what those right things are." After a few more sips of green tea, Sally asked Kristine to share her thoughts.

"Creating a success formula requires one to become intimate with their business activities," Kristine said. "Often, when I am coaching individuals, they say, 'I am so busy. I don't understand why I'm not making sales.'"

"Being a good coach," Sally said, "I like to ask my advisors a lot of questions, such as 'What isn't working?' 'Tell me about your sales process.' 'What is preventing you from having success?' 'What would you be willing to do differently to get better results?' "Far too often, advisors aren't even able to tell me what they did last week, so they have trouble answering these questions. One guarantee we can make is that if other people have had success, they can too. The truth is that everything can work when you work at it."

"I suggest that we start by analyzing the activities that an advisor is doing in a given day. We then broaden it to the week. Sometimes the advisor is so lost and distracted, we must start them with an activity journal to log their activities every hour for five days. This is a great way to become accountable to your time and intimate with your activities. Once you know what activities are being done, you can start to sort and classify them into larger categories. You may also suggest to completely remove some activities and put crucial activities in their place. Does that sound like a good starting point, Kristine?"

"Sally," Kristine replied, "how do we decide which activities to keep and lose?" They both thought for a moment. Then Kristine interjected. "It's simple. They must be activities that produce a paycheck. When I am coaching, I ask advisors to list all the activities that they do in a day. Then I ask them to tell me which ones are within two degrees of income generation. It may seem easy to decide which ones produce an income. Surprisingly, it's not. I ask the question 'How long do you think it will be before you see some income from this activity?' I agree that all activities are important, but the ones that must be completed first are the ones that are going to pay the bills this month."

"Perfect description, Kristine," Sally said. "Doing what is going to allow us to pay our bills this month is a great starting point. Let's identify activities now as they relate to our advisors.

1. **Prospecting** — leads to a sales presentation, which then leads to a closing appointment

2. **Fact Finding** — leads to an opportunity to provide solutions, which leads to a closing appointment

3. **Booking Appointments** — leads to a sales presentation, which leads to a closing appointment

"Now it is easy to see how all these income-generating activities are within two degrees of income generation. Let's review a few activities that are in our daily actions but may not be within two degrees of income generation.

1. **Education** — Although essential in creating future opportunity, it is not considered an income-generating activity by itself.

2. **Meetings with the Sales Team** — Meetings are essential in our business, but managing time spent in meetings (and how effective they are) will affect the time you have to create new sales opportunities.

3. **Networking** — Without an intent to follow up and take immediate action, networking is a soft form of marketing. A specific outcome that can lead to a sale must be within two degrees of income generation.

"So the first element of our success formula is income-generating activities."

"Yes, absolutely!" Kristine agreed.

Success Formula

Income-Generating Activities + _____ = _____

We would like to invite you, the reader, to complete your list of income-generating activities on the worksheet at the end of this chapter. This will assist you in becoming focused on the activities that should take priority in your business.

ACTING WITH INTENTION!

THE SECRET TO REDEFINING YOUR SUCCESS!

STEP 1: IDENTIFY YOUR ACTIVITIES. EVALUATE THEM AND CHOOSE THOSE THAT ARE WITHIN 2 DEGREES OF GENERATING INCOME:

In the left column you will brainstorm ALL of the activities you perform in a given day. The first part of this process is meant to be completely non-bias, a brainstorm of sorts. This exercise may not be as simple as it looks. Obviously, you KNOW you are busy! .... But doing what? If this is you, then you will need to take 1 or 2 full days where you keep an activity journal and document your activities each hour.

Once the activities are listed, you will now critically examine them. Only those that are within 2 degrees of earning money are permitted to go across to the short list.

DAILY ACTIVITIES	INCOME GENERATING ACTIVITIES. (Choose top 5)
	→
	→
	→
	→
	→

SIX

NEXT STEP—DEBATE

"**K**ristine, we have now identified the first step in our success formula. What's next?" Sally asked. "Do you think that if advisors simply focus on the right tasks, they will have success?"

"Without question, Sally. What we focus on, we create," Kristine said. "Tangible activities make this obvious and second nature. Take building a puzzle for example. We see a picture of what the end product looks like, take stock of the pieces we will need, analyze the contents of the box, and then start putting pieces together."

"Next, look at how the order of these activities matters—one at a time," Sally continued. "In our businesses, we are using the exact same concept. With the above-mentioned puzzle example, this process is obvious to a twelve-year-old, but in our businesses, we seem to lose this clarity. We must first choose the ending we want to produce, create our own picture of what success will look like—like the image on the puzzle box—and then keep that picture alive in our day-to-day activities."

Earlier, we identified our income-generating activities. Our next task is to attach them to our goals.

Success Formula

Income-Generating Activities + Serve Your Goals =_____

We all have different perspectives on what success looks like. Regardless of how we measure it, it's important that we focus on things that are important to us. People are driven by unique outcomes. For some, goals may be financial; for others, it may be taking their family on that dream vacation. It may take the form of being well respected in the community for the work they do, or it can be as simple as winning prizes or trophies.

"Kristine," Sally said, "when you came into your first year in financial services, your goal was to earn $100,000 or more in your first year. Your goal was clear and time-bound. How often do we have to remind advisors of the goals they set in their business plans? So often it is tucked in the back of a drawer or lost in a binder on a shelf—out of sight, out of mind. Most advisors not only are unclear about their goals but also don't believe they can achieve them. Another group may have only an idea of what they'd be willing to settle for."

"Many of our new advisors aren't brave enough to go for their dreams and be clear about how they will get there," Kristine added, shaking her head. "Being specific about our goals demands that we be accountable to them. The more tangible they are, the more real they are. Out of fear, many people lie to themselves about what the outcome will be and then believe the lie. Our best advice on goal setting is that, first, you have got to take the time to set them. Once goals are set, do a self-check to be sure they follow the following criteria.

1. **They must be specific.** No fluff and puff. No smoke and mirrors. Don't play games with yourself or those around you. Say it like you mean it, and be specific about it. Don't be a flakey goal setter. Own it.

2. **Make a commitment to a timeline.** It isn't okay to create a back door or a plan B right from the start. Be a person of your word. Don't let yourself off the hook. You are the most important person in your life. Be truthful and loyal to that person. If you can't stay committed to yourself and your own timelines, how can you be dependable to

others? How many times do you hear that someone got engaged but had no wedding date in mind? I stop asking 'When is the big day?' when I am repeatedly told they don't have one. I stop believing it will ever happen. Have you made a date for *your* big day? What is that *big* day that you have set to hit your goal in your business this year?

3. **Make the necessary sacrifices.** The sacrifice must equal the goal. Often people don't want to change anything about their lifestyle to achieve something. Let me share some news with you. To hit an extraordinary goal, you will have to knock the concept of life balance into a bit of a kilter for a while. Seriously, why is everyone so worried about 'balance' these days? Our word for that is *comfort*. We can have work–life balance, but large goals need time and attention. *Plan* when the right time is to sacrifice balance for that stretch goal and own the process for a committed amount of time. Try not to do these stretch goals at the same time as your partner. I look at my home life and partnership with my husband as a pendulum. Sometimes I carry the weight of balance, and sometimes he does. These agreements are formed in the planning

stages, so everyone knows what to expect. Don't try to be a superhero. Commit to the sacrifices. Inform those around you of the sacrifice and the timeline. Show gratitude when it is over and pick up balance once again.

4. **Goals must be kept in front of you.** They must be talked about with others and thought about each day. Visual reminders are important, and verbally expressing them is super powerful. A thought is just a thought until it is made real to other people in your circle. If you are not willing to write your goals down and tell others about them, then you likely don't believe they are real yourself. You certainly don't believe you will reach them if you don't talk about them. If you *can* reach goals that you have never spoken of, you are drastically underachieving. Most of your success will lie in your commitment to writing goals down, making the plan, and talking about them each day to your coach or peers."

Sally giggled and said to Kristine, "I know you are really big on goals. I agree this is a very important piece to our formula. It is not a secret that goals are important, but part of our challenge will be getting the advisors to keep their goals in front of them."

We would like to invite you to complete your goals on the worksheet at the end of this chapter. This will assist you in becoming focused on the goals that will keep you focused in your business.

ACTING WITH INTENTION!

THE SECRET TO REDEFINING YOUR SUCCESS!

STEP 2: Attach your Income Generating activities to a goal.

Although it is important to set goals in all goal areas, this exercise focuses only on career goals. Think about your goals for the next year. Next, break them down.

You will find that there are income generating goals and Non-income generating goals as well. Perhaps you have a professional development goal. Although these goals are notable and important, they do not take priority over an income generating goal.

LONG TERM (1 YEAR)	SHORT TERM (6 MOS)	BREAKING IT DOWN WEEKLY:	NARROW IT DOWN DAILY:

SEVEN

It's Got to be Nonnegotiable

"Kristine," Sally said, "I really like the way that our success formula is developing. When we talk about sales success, it really does depend on the individual and the focus that they put on their daily nonnegotiable activities. Most people avoid the activities that will lead them to success, and I often wonder why. When we bring in new advisors, they like to immerse themselves into training, ordering brochures and playing with new software but avoid what's really going to generate income."

"I absolutely see this as well," Kristine said. "Sally, when I ask a new advisor what they need to get them to their sales goals, they ultimately reply, 'Well, I need to learn more.' 'I'm not sure what I should be doing.' 'How can I go talk to a client if I don't know everything about our products?' I believe that many new advisors become quite overwhelmed. Sometimes it's self-induced."

"I understand each of us has a different communication style, but in most cases, many don't have the confidence to talk to our clients until we feel we know all the details inside and out," Sally explained. "Kristine, what our advisors don't understand is that after having studied and becoming licensed, they obviously know more than most clients will ever know. It's just a matter of focusing on sales activities that help you have the largest understanding of what the clients are truly looking for. We also understand that being in front of the client is where the biggest education comes from. You could know all technical information about the advisor role, but without having appointments with people, you as an advisor will be out of the business fast. When we first bring an advisor into our business, demonstrating the sales process is critical when the client is in front of both of you—the coach and the advisor."

"I love helping my new advisors with their sales process and show them the selling process," Kristine said. "What I found is if I demonstrate a simple repeatable process and the advisor embraces it, then they will have very fast success. It's when they believe that they need to change that simple repeatable process into something more complex that they start struggling. Every sales business that I've been in has had a sales cycle. It includes clearly defined steps on the process to follow through the sales cycle, including the meeting with a client."

"Why they fail in sales is the question that I have too." Sally expressed. "In my experience, people choose not to follow a sales process that is effective and proven over time. It's when advisors come in with a preconceived notion of what they feel the client is looking for that the sales process goes off track. I like to call that sales breath. When we just focus on what we believe we can sell to that client, we start planning what we're going to say to convince that person they need to purchase. I find that most of my new advisors all head down the path at some point in their first year, typically sooner than later. Why do they follow this path? Why did they get off track?"

"It truly comes from their heart," Kristine said emphatically, "as they believe that's what the client needs, and therefore, in an advisor's head, they have already completed the sale. Those blindfolds are back on and prevent them from seeing what the client is really wanting. The most powerful question in any sales appointment is handled at the beginning of the presentation, after developing rapport, when you ask the client, 'What were you hoping to achieve by the end of this appointment?' This is when the magic starts to happen. Why is this so powerful? Because the client gets to set their own agenda, and it allows an advisor to hear specifically what the client is looking for. In my experience, this is one of the hardest elements for a new advisor to embrace."

"So, Kristine," Sally said, "let me give you an example. As an insurance advisor, I may have been prospecting and found somebody interested in having their mortgage insured because I found out they have mortgage covered through their bank. Now as an insurance advisor, I know the value of having life insurance protection on that mortgage as opposed to creditor insurance, so immediately, I jump to the conclusion that this is a good prospect. When we meet in my office and I don't ask him an opening question, it's very easy for me to say, 'We met on Tuesday, and you mentioned that you have mortgage insurance, so I'd like to talk to you today about how life insurance is much more appropriate for your situation than what you currently own.'"

"When I approach a client in this fashion," Kristine interjected, "I often notice how the client's body language quickly changes. They cross their arms and sit back in their chair, and their responses get shorter. I keep trying to sell them on this concept as to why they need it. I might even go so far as to give them a quote, but at the end of the appointment, typically, the client leaves without purchasing a product from me. On the other hand, when I approach clients in a meeting and I ask them what the purpose was for them to see me, they will tell me exactly why they came in and what they're interested in learning about. How powerful is that for me as an advisor to be able to determine quickly what it is that the client is looking for? It gives me permission to ask clarifying questions about their need. In this situation, I have so much more engagement. I have clients who are asking me questions. I can now guide the sales process in a direction that will make the clients feel not only comfortable but also informed. And at the end of the meeting, the chances of closing a sale are much better than when I set the agenda for the client. Therefore, you and I have to create this successful formula, Sally. When we coach about our daily nonnegotiable activities, we can take our advisors in the right direction with their sales appointments and activities that drive our success."

"I have a really cool story to share, Kristine," Sally exclaimed. "When I started in the financial industry over a decade ago, I had a very successful advisor who had been in the business for over twenty years. When I would go to his office in the morning to greet him, he would have a sticky note in front of him, so one day I asked him why it was there. He responded that every morning, before ten o'clock, he had to speak to at least five clients, or five potential clients, before he could do any other activities in his day. If he didn't complete that task by ten o'clock, he would keep going until he did complete it. So why did he do this? Because those were his daily nonnegotiable activities. He knew that he had to complete those five conversations with clients or prospects every morning before he did anything else. It would create the success he needed to keep this business going. They *served his goals*. Daily nonnegotiable activities, when combined with your goals, will get you closer to success. The key is to really take the time to determine what those daily nonnegotiable activities are for that individual. They may feel painful at the beginning, but once they become a habit, they become quite easy to achieve on a daily basis."

Success Formula

Income-Generating Activities + Serve Your Goals = Daily Nonnegotiable Activities

"Sally, I love it!" Kristine said with excitement! "Now in comes the discipline. It has taken us a good amount of time to journal our activities and classify the ones that are income-generating. Next, we took the time to decide where we want to be by setting goals and planned out how we would get there. With this came conversations about our timelines and our agreed-upon sacrifices. We have even made these goals tangible by writing them down and telling other people about them. It is now time to label these income-generating activities that serve our goals as nonnegotiable.

"These are the activities that, moving forward in the distractions of day-to-day life, we will never toss aside. These activities must be done first before all others. Daily nonnegotiable activities are a double-edged sword. They keep the process simple and yet can be painful. These are always going to be the activities that bring the largest results and, therefore, cause the most discomfort or pain. Therefore, they require discipline and tend to be the activities advisors don't want to do. But if they allow themselves to leave them undone routinely, they will find themselves without an income or eventually without a career.

"Sally, I like to think of daily nonnegotiable activities as a car. I know that I won't move closer to my goals if I don't do the actions. This car drives me to my success.

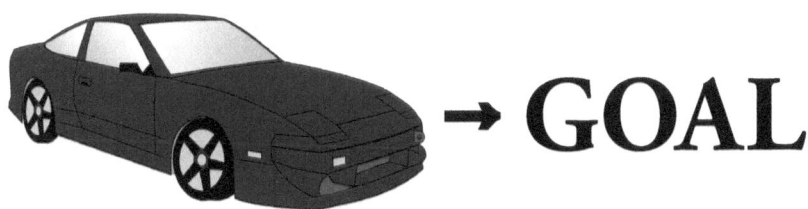 → GOAL

"There is another double-edged aspect of daily nonnegotiable activities—they cause pain, *but* they also reduce stress. It is like that therapeutic massage."

"That's funny, Kristine." Sally laughed. "But I completely understand this analogy. That reminds me I should make my massage appointment."

"Remember earlier," Kristine recounted, "when I talked about being in a company in constant change, Sally? I felt so out of control. In the financial industry, there are also many things that I cannot control, like whether a client holds their appointment without rescheduling or whether a client is insurable. I can't control all the technology changes, economic fluctuations, or regulatory changes. The list goes on and on. What I *can* control are my daily nonnegotiable activities. Because my clients are people with free will, I can never anticipate what decisions they may make, but I can control the activities that drive the results. I receive my confidence from the daily nonnegotiable activities that I accomplish. On Friday night, regardless of what happened that week, I feel great. I know that I served my goals all week. When I keep swinging, eventually, I will hit the ball."

We would like to invite you, the reader, to complete your list of daily nonnegotiable activities on the worksheet at the end of this chapter. This will assist you in becoming focused on the activities that should take top priority each day.

ACTING WITH INTENTION!

THE SECRET TO REDEFINING YOUR SUCCESS!

STEP 3: Non-negotiables! Identify which Income Generating Activities from step 1 Serve your goals.

Here it is important that your income generating activities are serving your goals. You may decide to do a separate chart for each goal. Don't focus on more than 3 goals.

These are your Non-Negotiable activities. All these activities must happen first in your day or week. Other activities still need to be done, but they must wait. The non-negotiables take priority.

INCOME GENERATING ACTIVITY	GOALS	NON-NEGOTIABLE
→	→	
→	→	
→	→	

EIGHT

REV UP YOUR ENGINES

"Kristine," Sally said, "I have worked with advisors who have set goals, identified their income-generating activities, and have decided on the ones that are daily nonnegotiable activities. But they *still* don't always do the activities consistently. In fact, at times, they even seem disengaged. How can we encourage them to keep going?"

"Well, remember the car analogy?" Kristine replied. "This car filled with daily nonnegotiable activities needs fuel to run. Let's imagine that I have a goal or destination in mind. I want to go from Texas to California in my car and have even packed up my car with all the supplies I will need. I start out the journey with a sense of fun and excitement. Eventually though, my car starts to putter somewhere on the long trip, and it can even slow to a stop at times. Suddenly, I am not going anywhere as I have run out of fuel. This happens so often in our businesses. Advisors may start out with great intensity and racing with enthusiasm, but they can start to 'tire out.' Why do you think that is?"

"I've got this one, Kristine." Sally interjected. "They must be *intentional*. They must connect with their personal intentions in achieving their goals. It is our intentions, our passions, that fuel this vehicle. Without being connected to our intentional outcomes, we will never finish the race we set for ourselves. Your journey will take you in the direction of your focus. If I look right, then I will drive to the right. If I look left, I will drive to the left. What we are intentional about, we create. By using the success formula, our advisors keep looking straight ahead."

Success Formula

Income-Generating Activities + Serve Your Goals = Daily Nonnegotiable Activities

Daily Nonnegotiable Activities + Intention = *Success*

"When you combine your daily nonnegotiable activities with your intention, you will achieve success!"

= SUCCESS

Nonnegotiable Intention

"Sally," Kristine said, "you knew that when I started as an advisor, my goal was to earn $100,000 or more per year. That goal was not just created because I like that number. It is because I have three daughters in elite sports, which is very pricey. Our eldest daughter is in pursuit of her Olympic dream. Haley is on the senior national ice dance team for Canada. When she was five years old, she told me that she wanted to be in the Olympics. From that day forward, I promised Haley that we would support her dream. There is no way that I will ever break it. I have a clear intention in my heart."

"When working with our advisors," Sally added, "it may seem like a simple concept to talk about their intentions. It can be one of the toughest aspects of the success formula. Like peeling back an onion, you may even get a few tears. Often people are not aware of their own core intentions. It takes some effort to dig down through the different layers to distinguish what the driving forces really are."

"I've always been a huge believer in being intentional!" Kristine exclaimed. "This is a word that I'm known for. It is something that comes naturally to me in pretty much every role in my life. Sally, you and I sit and talk about this a lot. Being intentional is a result of keeping your word to your clients, keeping your word to yourself, and keeping your word to those you are accountable to. Acting with intention is an act of good character. It drives our motivations and creates passion. As you and I have been working with our advisors, we have noticed that if we keep our conversations strictly to activities, we don't get the results. We have found greater results when we are willing to dig a little deeper and investigate the human side of what motivates those whom we are working with. I think it's easy as a coach to fall into the trap of just sticking to company goals in our conversations."

"Some people love earning prizes," Sally continued, "but not everyone. This actually shocked me early in my mentorship endeavors. I thought everyone liked rewards. So how can we keep campaigns exciting for as many as possible? For some, to reach their goals, we must figure out what it is that will drive the passion and the energy to get that advisor where they need to go. Often advisors are strictly hearing about targets. And many feel they are 'put on them' and, therefore, don't feel a sense of ownership around them. It can create a divide between the advisors and the leadership team."

"This divide is easily broken, though, if we can reach the heart of what drives that individual. We don't have to be psychologists or counselors. We just need to ask the right questions. Someone in our company once gave me a phrase that I love to use. The phrase is 'Tell me more about that.' I love that phrase because it starts to encourage those I am working with to elaborate. It is good to watch them get nervous. I think we tend to be much too comfortable taking things at face value. Asking the right questions can be uncomfortable and yet *so* powerful."

As Sally and Kristine talked about strategies in helping in a very professional way, they decided it was quite simple. They decided to just use that small three-letter word *why* all the time with advisors. The concept of asking the five why's to get to the heart of the issue is so impactful. They started using it more than once, more than twice, more than even three times in coaching conversations, and they discovered how powerful that little word can be.

Finding the personal intentions and motivations of an individual not only enables us to fuel activities and increase motivation but also improves our relationships because our advisors feel valued. Many times, after they repeatedly ask why, their final answers surprise them. It's a part of the process of removing the blindfold. The success formula allows us to really help our advisors discover and own their intentions. When we work with intention, it is like a fire in their belly that drives them to achieve success.

In our office, we both work with senior advisors. Ron is one of our twenty-five-plus-years advisors. He's built a very successful practice and takes great pride in how he has helped his clients over the years.

"In partnering with Ron," Sally shared, "I discovered that he was really struggling with his succession plan. He had explored many paths, including partnerships with other advisors, some young and some tenured. He thought about teaming up in an alliance with another advisor who had the infrastructure in their administrative team that he desired. He admired a new advisor who had qualified for MDRT in his first three years and started planning succession with his team. Yet none of these options were giving Ron exactly what he desired. As a matter of fact, Ron does not like change. He is happy with his processes, his office location, his relationships with his clients, and his team.

"As I started to work with Ron through his process, I noticed that he had a lot of unrest and his sales results were declining. Of course, he insisted it was because he was so busy doing retirement plans for his clients that he didn't have time for selling new products. It was time to peel back the onion. So layer by layer, I discovered that Ron was not adopting the new planning tools that our organization had provided that would save him a tremendous amount of time. I also discovered that he had a lot of anxiety as the time was approaching for the retirement date of his trusted long-term assistant. He is also not keen on training a new assistant. Ron also wanted more time off to visit his grown children who had moved all over the world to work. Deep down, I discovered that Ron was so distracted by the *change* in his world that he couldn't focus on present-day targets.

"So the first step was to get Ron back on track with his daily nonnegotiables. We trained him on our planning tool, which empowered him to not only find the time in his day to complete his retirement plans but also identify sales opportunities. Ron was back on track in a short time from a sales perspective. We all know that senior advisors know how to sell. He was just overwhelmed.

"The challenge remained on his succession plan. Now this allowed me to really peel back the onion on his intentions. Every day Ron would pop by my office at the end of the day with another solution, idea, or 'what if' scenario. I knew we needed to apply the success formula. I decided to dig into his intention by using the five whys. We knew that he needed a gradual succession plan, but this exercise helped him get clarity.

"*Why?* So he could balance his personal time off with his business.

"*Why?* He had been successful and wanted to stay in the business.

"*Why?* Because he loves what he does, especially the relationships he built up.

"*Why?* Impact in his community was extremely important to Ron.

"*Why?* He wanted someone to take over his business who would uphold his reputation in the community.

"*Bingo!* We now had his *true intention*. Ron has lived in this community his whole life. He has been a very reputable contributing member in the area. His main concern would be how others would perceive his choice of successor. How fun it was to really find out how to not only get Ron back on track but also assist him in finding the *perfect* successor in the community.

"I'm happy to report that all has worked out for Ron. He is having a work–life balance, his sales have increased, and he now has a succession plan that he *loves*. When you combine your daily nonnegotiables with your intention, you will achieve success. I know that you have some great stories as well, Kristine, on how our success formula has worked. How about Kyli?"

Kristine started, "I brought this amazing young woman into the business, very focused and energetic. She had all the qualities that I look for in a great new advisor, and Kyli had a very strong start. By about the third month, I noticed that her sales had really slowed down. When I talked with her, it sounded like she had started focusing on activities that were not serving the goals that she had written about in her business plan. I decided right there she needed an intervention.

"I pulled Kyli aside for a meeting. Although she expressed that her goals and intentions had not changed, all her activities had changed and weren't aligning with her intentions. Kyli's income was quickly decreasing, and her stress levels were rising. She was telling me that she was questioning her decision to be an advisor with our company. I immediately decided that Kyli needed to revisit her success formula. We needed to get her car back on course. She was headed down the wrong road.

"I asked her, 'What are your intentions?' and 'What are your goals?'"

"She expressed an income goal, and I asked her, 'Why?' and then 'Why?' again and then 'Why?' again until she finally disclosed that she was a competitive barrel racer and must be able to care for her three barrel horses. Kyli was afraid that she would have to give her horses up if she couldn't make enough money to support them. Her intention became very clear. Failure was not an option.

"Kyli and I worked through the processes of the success formula. We agreed upon her new success formula because she was already disciplined and understood the daily habits of training her horses. She quickly adopted this formula as a way of life. She repeats the daily nonnegotiable activities each week and forms a habit. *Success!* Kyli makes a quick turnaround. She is our top new advisor in the current campaign, and her income exceeds her goal. The difference between people who succeed and those who fail are the ones who make their success formula into a habit. Once it becomes a habit, the fear diminishes."

Success Formula

Income-Generating Activities + Serve Your Goals = Daily Nonnegotiable Activities

Daily Nonnegotiable Activities + Intention = *Success*

We would like to invite you, the reader, to peel back your own onion to get to your true intention on the worksheets at the end of this chapter. This will assist you in understanding how to achieve success as you create your success formula.

ACTING WITH INTENTION!

THE SECRET TO REDEFINING YOUR SUCCESS!

STEP 4: Peel back the onion by drilling down with your long-term goal:

We need to fuel these goals by getting down to the heart of each matter. Your intentions are your own unique motivators. A good coach will always work to help team members use their passion and desire to bring energy and joy to the tasks.

GOAL 1.	GOAL 2.	GOAL 3.
WHY?	WHY?	WHY?
WHY?	WHY?	WHY?
WHY?	WHY?	WHY?
WHY?	WHY?	WHY?
INTENTION	INTENTION	INTENTION

"To be intentional is to act purposefully, with a goal in mind and a plan for accomplishing it." Anne Epstein

STEP 5: Create your SUCCESS FORMULA!

ACTING WITH INTENTION!

THE SECRET TO REDEFINING YOUR SUCCESS!

Step 5: Now we are ready to put all these unique pieces together.

Daily Non-Negotiables   +   Weekly Non-Negotiables   +   Be Intentional!

1._____   1. _____

Write a short paragraph expressing why you will commit to these Non-negotiables. Include the sacrifice you will make:

2._____   2. _____

3._____   3. _____

4._____   4. _____

5._____   5. _____

Success, Defined by Me! In one year, I see myself:

_____

_____

_____

_____

_____

_____

_____

"Our goals can only be reached through a vehicle of a plan, in which we must fervently believe, and upon which we must vigorously act. There is no other route to success." – Pablo Picasso

Our goals can only be reached through a vehicle of a plan in which we must fervently believe and upon which we must vigorously act. There is no other route to success.

— Pablo Picasso

NINE

SHORTEN TIME TO SUCCESS

"Kristine," Sally cheerfully said, "I'm so happy with our success formula and the fun we had together in fine-tuning it to create success. The results that we are experiencing with our advisors are incredible. Earlier, we spoke about the many changes in our industry and in the world. It is so easy to become distracted. It was interesting to be able to address these changes by facing them with innovation and ideas that look at the opportunities ahead of us in a different way."

"Every business, including our industry, is facing challenges to keep itself relevant to the consumer," Kristine added. "For the business to keep learning and growing at the pace needed, many fundamentals of our business may get ignored. Sometimes we start looking for that new magic trick that will expedite our success, maybe in the form of new software or social media. While we are making the effort to keep up with all these changes, the answers to success are right in front of us. The human aspect of doing business still exists, and our proven success formula will keep one laser-focused during any storm. As advisors work with their personal success formula, they will find that it will evolve and change with them."

"If advisors are like you and me," Sally expressed, "as a mentor, coach, or recruiter, the success formula will allow them to select the right people, identify when they skid off the road, and see success much faster than in the past. Long-term success in our industry depends on retention and production. Getting new advisors to develop a success formula will shorten their time to success and help them get through those critical first two years. Being intimate with oneself and their personal businesses, staying true to core intentions, making sacrifices, and being committed to the journey—the success formula is an anchor in the storm of change, and it can work for everyone."

"The worksheets that we have made available make this process simple," Kristine shared. "They will guide others through the step-by-step process of creating a personalized success formula. The journey connects the human aspect of business to the functional activities that are necessary to achieve success. Whatever our roles—advisor, manager, trainer, or CEO—each of us plays a part in making an impact on the future success of our sales teams in this ever-changing industry."

Success Formula

Income-Generating Activities + Serve Your Goals = Daily Nonnegotiable Activities

Daily Nonnegotiable Activities + Intention = *Success*

This success formula involves both *action* and intention.

Don't be thrown off your game. Act now, and act with intention— the secret to redefining your success!

www.ingramcontent.com/pod-product-compliance
Lightning Source LLC
Chambersburg PA
CBHW030857180526
45163CB00004B/1609